SUPERSTARS

of

PRO FOOTBALL

BRIAN WESTBROOK

David Robson

Mason Crest Publishers

Produced by OTTN Publishing in association with
21st Century Publishing and Communications, Inc.

MASON CREST PUBLISHERS INC.
370 Reed Road
Broomall, Pennsylvania 19008
(866) MCP-BOOK (toll free)
www.masoncrest.com

Printed in the United States of America.

First Printing

9 8 7 6 5 4 3 2 1

Library of Congress Cataloging-in-Publication Data

Robson, David W.
  Brian Westbrook / David Robson.
    p. cm. — (Superstars of pro football)
  Includes bibliographical references and index.
ISBN-13: 978-1-4222-0547-1 — ISBN-10: 1-4222-0547-9
ISBN-13: 978-1-4222-0839-7 (pbk.) — ISBN-10: 1-4222-0839-7 (pbk.)
  1. Westbrook, Brian, 1979–   —Juvenile literature. 2. Running backs (Football)—
United States—Biography—Juvenile literature. 3. Philadelphia Eagles (Football
team)—Juvenile literature. I. Title.
GV939.W47R63 2008
796.332092—dc22
[B]   2008031072

◀◀ CROSS-CURRENTS ▶▶

In the ebb and flow of the currents of life we are each influenced
by many people, places, and events that we directly experience or
have learned about. Throughout the chapters of this book you will
come across **CROSS-CURRENTS** reference bubbles. These bubbles
direct you to a **CROSS-CURRENTS** section in the back of the
book that contains fascinating and informative sidebars
and related pictures. Go on. ▶▶

◀◀CONTENTS▶▶

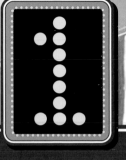

A SECRET NO LONGER

At one time, Philadelphia Eagles running back Brian Westbrook was the National Football League's best-kept secret. Quiet and reserved by nature, Brian does not dance in the end zone or hold press conferences to flaunt his considerable achievements. Instead, he does his job and lets his accomplishments speak for him.

On December 18, 2007, the secret was revealed as Brian Westbrook was chosen to play in the NFL Pro Bowl—the league's annual all-star game, held in Honolulu, Hawaii. He had taken the trip before, but this time was different. In 2005 Brian had been a second alternate for the game, but only because two other star running backs withdrew due to injury. Now, for the

Brian Westbrook of the Philadelphia Eagles has emerged as one of the NFL's premier running backs. A quick, shifty runner, Brian is also an excellent receiver. His versatility causes headaches for opponents' defenses.

CROSS-CURRENTS

Each year, the NFL's best players gather in Honolulu for the Pro Bowl, played on the Sunday after the Super Bowl. For a history of the all-star game, see page 46. ▶▶

first time in his career, the Eagles' powerhouse running back was voted in by NFL coaches and his fellow football players. The day of the announcement, Brian spoke of his feelings:

"When you're getting voted to go play in an all-star game by your peers and the other coaches, it definitely validates you as a player. I hope that people will continue to see the things that I can bring to a football team and see the things I can help a football team be. Hopefully, that will continue and my good play will continue as well."

In the Beginning

From the beginning of his NFL career in 2002, Brian has set himself apart, content to work hard at practice during the week before confusing defenses and dazzling fans on Sunday afternoon. With little fanfare, he takes the handoff, tucks the football, ducks his head, and plunges forward. But when Brian Westbrook carries the ball, jaws drop. The Eagles' Web site officially lists Brian at five feet ten, although that may overestimate his height by an inch or two. And at just over 200 pounds—all of it muscle—Brian is small compared to some of the enormous, man-eating NFL linemen he faces. In fact, when he joined the Eagles in 2002, broadcasters and players alike wondered whether the rookie back was big enough, strong enough, and tough enough to make it in the hard-hitting, bone-crunching world of professional football. But Brian used the doubts and low expectations to fuel his athletic performance. By doing so, he racked up spectacular numbers both on the ground and through the air.

Since his second year in the league, no other running back in the NFL has gained more receiving yards—3,207, on 347 receptions. As a rusher Brian has chalked up 4,785 yards, and he averages a whopping 4.7 yards per carry. He leads his team in career touchdowns with 50. On the field he is a team leader; off the field he encourages teammates and the thousands of young people he meets to do their best and never stop working.

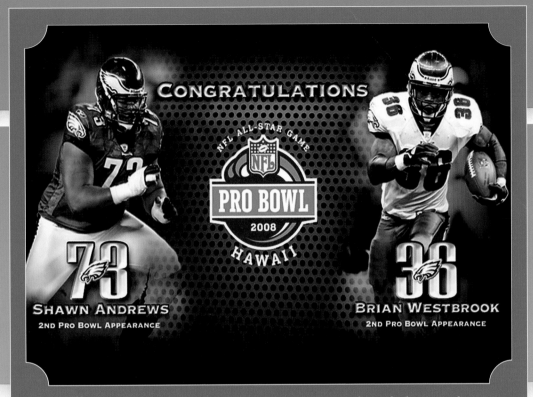

CONGRATULATIONS

PRO BOWL 2008
NFL ALL-STAR GAME
HAWAII

73
SHAWN ANDREWS
2ND PRO BOWL APPEARANCE

36
BRIAN WESTBROOK
2ND PRO BOWL APPEARANCE

In 2007 Brian Westbrook led all NFL players in total yards from scrimmage (rushing and receiving). His stellar performance landed Brian on the NFC's 2008 Pro Bowl roster. Offensive guard Shawn Andrews was the only other Eagle selected for the all-star game.

Still, despite the statistics and the praise he earns for his drive, Brian rarely speaks of his notable skills as a runner and receiver. Unlike the professional athletes who enjoy bragging about their feats or taunting their opponents, Brian is content to let his actions speak for him. But he does appreciate it when others notice his talent.

Super Duper

In January 2008, as the New York Giants prepared to meet the New England Patriots in Super Bowl XLII, the humble Brian Westbrook came out of his shell. He was ready for his close-up. So while the **media** swarmed Giants and Patriots players, Brian also took a turn at the microphone. He spoke with pride of the respect he had gained from other players in his six-year NFL career:

> **"I think the more they notice you, the more they want to be around you. I definitely appreciate that guys notice my play on the field, and I appreciate that guys respect that as well."**

Although disappointed that his Birds were not playing in the big game, the scrappy back took it in stride. His awe-inspiring numbers during the 2007 season were some consolation. During a lackluster

Would-be tackler Josh Bullocks is left grasping air after a Brian Westbrook move, December 23, 2007. Brian rushed for 100 yards on the day, helping his Eagles defeat the New Orleans Saints, 38–23.

season for the team, Brian broke an Eagles **franchise** record and led the National Football League in yards from scrimmage: combined, his running and receiving yards totaled 2,104.

From his early days playing for Villanova University to his dazzling performances on the field with the Eagles, the quiet man has become one of the NFL's foremost double threats. He can run and he can catch. Best of all, however, he can make tacklers miss.

Yet, personal accolades are secondary to this Maryland native. What he really desires is a Super Bowl ring to add to his collection of trophies and plaques. His hard-charging, defender-dodging abilities have helped carry the Philadelphia Eagles to NFC Champi-onships and a Super Bowl. And although the team has yet to win it all, it is not for Brian's lack of trying.

So in the days leading up to Super Bowl XLII, Brian remained hopeful that the Eagles would someday return to the big game—and that this time they would emerge victorious:

CROSS-CURRENTS

Brian Westbrook's on-field heroics and solid work ethic have made him a favorite of Eagles fans. For a look at these famously passion-ate fans, turn to page 47.

> **When I see the two teams playing in the Super Bowl that we've competed against very well—and we had an opportunity to beat both teams—it gives you that confidence that we can be here, as well as win this game.**

Brian Westbrook, the ultimate team player, knows that no player can travel the road to the Super Bowl alone. If football is truly a team sport, then perhaps Brian Westbrook should be its honorary captain.

DC TO THE MAIN LINE

Brian Collins Westbrook was born in Washington, D.C., on September 2, 1979. His parents, Zelda and Ronald Westbrook, raised their son in Fort Washington, Maryland. From an early age, Brian took an interest in basketball and football. But it was a fateful day in his eighth-grade year that would set the course for the rest of his life.

Brian was not especially big for his age, but he had proved his athletic talent playing Boys' Club football in his neighborhood. Now, coaches from one of most respected high schools in the country wanted to meet him. DeMatha Catholic High School's athletic program is consistently ranked in the top 10 in the United

States. During Brian's visit, players and coaches asked the quiet young man whether he would like to play football for DeMatha. Brian's answer was an enthusiastic yes.

High Flying in High School

For three years, Brian's mother drove him the 20 miles each way to DeMatha in Washington, D.C. There, he lettered in both football and basketball. In his senior year, he made first-team All-League. But his time there was not without disappointment and struggle. In the months before his senior year, Brian partially tore a ligament in his knee while dunking a basketball during a contest.

Brian Westbrook is by nature quiet and reserved, and as a youth he was never big for his age. His dazzling athletic talent, however, caught the eye of coaches at football powerhouse DeMatha Catholic High School in Washington, D.C.

Brian Westbrook's mother, Zelda—seen here at an event in Philadelphia for breast cancer survivors—is a regional coordinator for the Professional Football Players Mothers' Association. The association supports programs that help women and underprivileged children.

Throughout his ups and downs at DeMatha, Brian forged a special relationship with football coach Bill McGregor. McGregor is widely considered one of the best high school football coaches in the country, as former Washington Redskins head coach Joe Gibbs attested:

> **Bill McGregor and his assistant coaches are the best high school coaching staff in the country. Not only are they great coaches but more so, they are great teachers. No doubt they would do a great job at any level.**

McGregor saw in Brian Westbrook a modest and hard-working athlete who sacrificed everything for his team. As Brian's high school career came to an end, it was McGregor who always put in a good word for his young player. When colleges inquired about his star athlete over the phone, McGregor sometimes even added a few pounds and a few inches to Brian's size.

In 1997 Brian graduated with honors and a 3.6 grade point average from DeMatha Catholic High School. While his injuries might have discouraged lesser players, Brian was determined to continue playing football in college. He got the chance to do just that when Villanova University in Pennsylvania decided to take a chance on his smarts and athletic potential. It was a decision officials there would not regret.

Wildcats Calling

Brian Westbrook's move from a middle-class **suburb** of Washington, D.C., to the wealthy Philadelphia suburb of Villanova was the beginning of a new journey for the talented running back. The oldest—and, by the late 1990s, the largest Catholic University in Pennsylvania—Villanova is grounded in religious tradition. But it also boasts a prominent athletic program. The school has produced many stars of track and field. And in 1985 Villanova's men's basketball team won a national championship.

In 1997 Brian Westbrook entered Villanova, intent on continuing his athletic career. As a freshman for the Wildcats, Brian carried the football 97 times for 630 yards, averaging 6.5 yards per carry. During a game against Colgate, he returned a kickoff 89 yards for a touchdown, becoming only the seventh player in Villanova history to take a kickoff into the end zone.

Brian had found his groove by 1998. He became the first player in **NCAA** history to gain 1,000 yards rushing and 1,000 yards receiving in a single season. But just when it seemed as if Brian could not be stopped, injury put him down for the count. He spent the 1999 Villanova season on the sidelines because of a knee injury.

But a year later, he returned and burned up the turf. Brian broke the all-time NCAA career record with 9,512 all-purpose yards (rushes, pass receptions, kickoff returns, and punt returns). During his 46 career games at Villanova, Brian scored 84 touchdowns. Wildcats coach Andy Talley still speaks with awe about Brian Westbrook's talent:

An aerial view of Villanova Stadium, the scene of many great football performances by Brian Westbrook. Brian was the first player in NCAA history to gain 1,000 yards rushing and 1,000 yards receiving in a single season. He accomplished the feat in 1998.

> "He's an every-down back. He's tough enough to take the hitting, and he's always ducking under or sidestepping. No one gets a clean shot at him."

But Brian's **gridiron** greatness, surprisingly, did not translate into much interest from the NFL in 2002. Despite Talley's enthusiasm, many scouts still viewed Brian as too small and injury prone to make it in the hard-hitting world of professional football.

CROSS-CURRENTS

For information on the NFL draft—including great players who were, like Brian Westbrook, passed over by the experts— turn to page 48. ▶▶

Cat to Bird

One NFL coach did take a keen interest in Brian Westbrook. Philadelphia Eagles coach Andy Reid had closely watched Brian's progress on the field. Reid saw a talented athlete. He also saw a modest yet confident person off the field, a young man of character who could be a team leader. Reid believed Brian would fit in perfectly with his fast-improving team:

> "He's a heck of a football player. He does so many different things . . . so well, whether it's catching the football or running the football. When you're able to have that kind of balance with one player, there are not a lot of those guys in the National Football League."

Yet based on what Reid had been hearing, selecting Brian Westbrook in the 2002 draft was a gamble. Questions lingered: Could the back remain injury free? Could he take punishing hits, dust himself off, and rejoin the huddle? Could he make a positive contribution to the Eagles' offense? Like so many coaches, Reid relied on gut instinct, and his gut told him to draft Brian Westbrook. The Eagles selected Brian in the third round of the 2002 draft. Only time would tell whether Reid's gamble would pay off.

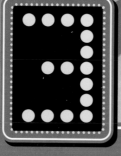

SMALL BUT TOUGH

The move from college to professional football can be challenging for any player. The offensive schemes are more complex, the stakes are higher, and the defenses are bigger. Though Brian Westbrook had spent four very successful seasons with Villanova, many football observers thought he was simply too small and too injury prone to become a star in the NFL.

Underestimated

Philadelphia Eagles head coach Andy Reid knew what it was like to be underestimated. Born in Los Angeles in 1958, Reid had played offensive guard and tackle at Brigham Young University in

Brian Westbrook at his first Philadelphia Eagles training camp. Small by the standards of NFL running backs, Brian was passed over until the third round of the 2002 NFL draft, when Philadelphia took him with the 91st overall pick.

Utah, graduating in 1981. For the next 10 years, he was an offensive-line coach at a succession of colleges.

In 1992 came his big break. The Green Bay Packers were hiring, and when Reid was offered an assistant coaching position he jumped at the chance to break into the NFL. The Packers were a storied franchise. They had won the first two Super Bowls, in 1967 and 1968.

Behind quarterback Brett Favre, the Packers also won Super Bowl XXXI in 1996. Two years later, Reid's work and reputation earned him the head coaching job with the Eagles. But like his future running back Brian Westbrook, many sportswriters—and many football executives—wondered whether he could make the leap to the big time.

Philadelphia Eagles head coach Andy Reid. Like his star running back, Reid is a modest, soft-spoken man. He is also the winningest coach in Eagles history.

Already Moving

By the time Brian Westbrook landed with the Eagles in 2002, the team was already on the move. Philadelphia had won only three games in 1998, but after just two seasons under Andy Reid, the team posted an 11–5 regular-season record and secured a spot in the playoffs. A year later, in 2001, the Eagles won the National Football Conference (NFC) East division and played in the NFC Championship game. Although they lost to the St. Louis Rams, 29–24, Reid's coaching won accolades. "He respects his players," Eagles linebacker Ike Reese noted. "He respects his leaders. He allows us and expects us to take owner- ship of the team. As players, we respect that."

Brian Westbrook got his first chance to prove himself during the 2002 season—his rookie year in the NFL. His play, however, was limited.

But the 2002 Eagles seemed poised to succeed without him. Running back Duce Staley kept the Eagles' **backfield** humming. The team finished the regular season with a division-best 12–4 record. In their first playoff game, the Eagles trounced the Atlanta Falcons, 20–3. On a frigid Sunday in January 2003, however, the Tampa Bay Buccaneers ruined the Birds' dreams of a Super Bowl. The Bucs rolled over the hometown Eagles, 27–10, in the NFC Championship game. As coach Andy Reid took one last look at the scoreboard, he was already wondering how he might use his running back from Villanova to help take the Eagles to the next level.

Three in the Backfield

For Brian Westbrook, training camp for the 2003 season was quite eventful. Starter Duce Staley was in the final year of his contract with the Eagles, and he failed to appear at the team's training camp in July. Staley hoped his holdout would persuade the team to sign him to a new and bigger contract. But Eagles owner Jeffrey Lurie and team president Joe Banner refused to change Staley's contract. When Staley eventually did return to the team, he found himself sharing running- back duties with Correll Buckhalter and Brian Westbrook.

Although Staley continued putting up good numbers, Brian Westbrook made a few waves himself, particularly during an October 19 game against the Eagles' NFC East rivals the New York Giants. With only 76 seconds left on the game clock and the Eagles down by three points, Brian stunned the men in blue—and his own teammates—by returning a New York punt 84 yards for a touchdown. The Eagles won the game, 14–10. Brian's return helped turn the season around.

Brian went on to score a total of 11 more touchdowns in his second season with the Birds. But in the team's final game, against the Washington Redskins, the scrappy back tore a triceps muscle in his upper arm and missed the playoffs. The Eagles again reached the NFC Championship game and again failed to win.

Brian Westbrook is on his way to the end zone with an 84-yard punt return against the New York Giants, October 23, 2003. Brian scored with just 76 seconds left in the game, giving the Eagles a 14–10 victory.

First-time Starter

Brian Westbrook became the Eagles' starting running back during the 2004 season. Staley had been traded to Pittsburgh and Correll Buckhalter went down with an injury to his knee. The big question was whether Brian could fill their shoes and help quarterback Donovan McNabb and the rest of the team make good on the promise of the previous season's playoff drive.

McNabb was fast becoming one of the best quarterbacks in the league. In 1999, when Philadelphia had used its first-round draft pick to take the Syracuse University star, some fans had booed. Many die-hard Eagles boosters had wanted the team to pick University of Texas running back Ricky Williams. But in his first season as a starter, McNabb came in second for Most Valuable Player honors. His powerful throwing arm was coupled with an uncanny ability to scramble and avoid sacks. Philadelphians quickly embraced McNabb as the key player in their Super Bowl dreams.

CROSS-CURRENTS

For a profile of Philadelphia Eagles quarterback Donovan McNabb, a perennial Pro Bowl selection, turn to page 49. ▶▶

Now Brian Westbrook was in a position to make a real difference on the football field. And from the start of the new season, Brian lived up to the potential Coach Reid had seen two years before. He rushed for 812 yards and, just as important, caught 73 passes for 703 yards. With McNabb hitting his targets and Brian confusing defenses—and with a gritty defense of its own—Philadelphia dominated opponents on both sides of the ball. The team ended the regular season with a 13–3 record. Their commanding playoff performances included a 27–14 pummeling of the Minnesota Vikings and, finally, an NFC Championship win over the Atlanta Falcons, 27–10.

For the first time since the 1980 season—and only the second time ever—the Eagles would play in the Super Bowl. Yet despite his performance during the regular season and the playoffs, Brian Westbrook continued to be underestimated. He was offered few endorsement deals during his first years in the league. He was quiet, small, and modest—a team player who considered his own individual statistics secondary to the success of the Eagles as a whole. Those qualities had helped the Eagles make it to the top. Now only one game remained: the Super Bowl XXXIX matchup in Jacksonville, Florida, against the tenacious and talented New

CROSS-CURRENTS

To read about the Philadelphia Eagles' first Super Bowl appearance, against the Oakland Raiders in 1981, go to page 50. ▶▶

England Patriots. New England's players and coaches didn't underestimate Brian Westbrook. They fully recognized how dangerous a weapon he was, as Patriots safety Rodney Harrison told a reporter a few days before the Super Bowl:

❝He creates so many mismatch problems because he is so quick and so fast. He has tremendous versatility. We have to make sure we know where he is at all times. He's going to make his share of plays, but we can't let him take a screen 60 yards to the house [end zone]. We have to have more than one guy tackle him.❞

Going to the Show

During the 2004 season Brian—despite his busy schedule of practice and play—had nominated his old DeMatha football coach Bill McGregor for the NFL's High School Coach of the Year. Based in part on Brian's high praise, McGregor won the award, which included a $5,000 prize for him and a $10,000 grant for DeMatha football, along with two tickets to the Super Bowl. When asked about his former coach before the big game, Brian responded:

❝He's been doing a great job in DeMatha for a long time. He taught me a lot. He's done a lot for me. So it's definitely an honor for him to be down here with me. I'm glad he was able to win the award.❞

As for Super Bowl XXXIX itself, the Eagles came ready to play. The men in green controlled the ball for much of the first half. Even so, they went into the locker room at halftime tied with the Patriots, 7–7.

The Patriots scored a touchdown on their first drive of the second half to take a 14–7 lead. Late in the third quarter, the Eagles struck back. Donovan McNabb hit Brian Westbrook with a pass over the middle, and Brian scampered 10 yards for a touchdown, capping a 10-play, 74-yard drive for the Eagles. Going into the fourth quarter, the game was tied. But it would not remain that way for long.

Brian Westbrook talks to reporters in Jacksonville, Florida, on February 1, 2005. Five days later, the Eagles would meet the New England Patriots in Super Bowl XXXIX.

Brian Westbrook runs through an arm tackle by New England Patriots cornerback Hank Poteat in first-half action from Super Bowl XXXIX, February 6, 2008. The game was closely contested, but New England pulled away early in the fourth quarter and hung on to win, 24–21.

New England scored a touchdown early in the final quarter, then added a field goal with 8:43 left on the clock, to go up by a score of 24–14. After a Patriots **interception** and a defensive stop by the Eagles, McNabb was back behind center. With only 5:40 left in the game, the dynamic quarterback led another touchdown drive, this time tossing a pass to wide receiver Greg Lewis. But though the Eagles kept the Patriots from scoring again, their hope gave out when

McNabb threw his third interception of the game in the closing moments. Final score: 24–21.

Wide receiver Terrell Owens, injured in the second half of the season, had put on a stunning performance, catching nine passes for 122 yards. McNabb had thrown for three touchdowns and more than 350 yards, but he had also been picked off three times. For Brian Westbrook, the most important game of his life had been neither glorious nor embarrassing: he caught seven passes for 60 yards and rushed for another 44 yards.

Nothing could erase the pain of losing the Super Bowl, but Brian could take some solace in his selection to the Pro Bowl. It was the first time in his young NFL career that Brian had received this honor.

Pay Day

Brian Westbrook's off-season was consumed with contract negotiations. By now the running back felt he had proved his worth to his team. But the negotiations dragged on into the summer of 2005, and Brian did not appear at the first week of training camp. In September, as the season began, talks between Brian's agent and the Eagles broke down. Brian had returned to the club, but he suggested that the team was disrespecting him.

Despite his frustration, Brian played hard, and the Eagles won three of their first four games. In early November, the team rewarded Brian with a five-year contract extension worth a reported $25 million. By this time, however, the season had begun to unravel for the NFC's defending champions. On November 6, halfway through the regular season, the team's record stood at a lackluster 4–4. Star wide receiver Terrell Owens had been suspended for publicly criticizing quarterback Donovan McNabb and the Eagles organization as a whole. A week later, injuries ended McNabb's season. Brian Westbrook hurt his foot, and had to miss the final four games of the season, in the Eagles' humiliating 42–0 loss to the Seattle Seahawks on December 6.

Without their three biggest offensive stars, the Eagles staggered to a 6–10 finish. Still, Brian Westbrook was happy with his new contract. And he was confident that, in 2006, the Birds would once again soar toward the Super Bowl.

WE CAN REBUILD HIM

A swollen knee made Brian Westbrook's return to the Birds' 2006 roster uncertain. But the determined running back would not give up. When the Eagles opened the regular season against the Houston Texans, Brian was in the lineup. He helped seal a victory for Philadelphia with a 31-yard touchdown reception.

In mid-November, in a game against the Tennessee Titans, McNabb went down with a season-ending knee injury. Brian took it upon himself to fill the leadership vacuum. In the locker room, he frequently rallied his teammates, and younger members of the team often went to him for guidance. On the field he excelled, picking up much of the slack created by McNabb's

power of one

As the 2006 season got under way, the Philadelphia Eagles were focused on one goal: making it back to the Super Bowl and bringing an NFL championship to the City of Brotherly Love.

Brian Westbrook eludes Washington Redskins safety Sean Taylor, November 12, 2006. Brian's 113 rushing yards and 37 receiving yards helped pace the Eagles to a 27–3 victory in the game.

absence. A week after McNabb's injury, Brian became only the second Eagle to rush for over 100 yards in three straight games. The first, Eagles legend Wilbert Montgomery, had done it in 1981.

CROSS-CURRENTS

Brian Westbrook has drawn comparisons with another all-time great Eagles running back: Wilbert Montgomery. For a profile of Montgomery, see page 51. ▶▶

Go-to Garcia

As a replacement for his Pro Bowl quarterback, Coach Reid looked to veteran Jeff Garcia. Garcia had played for the San Francisco 49ers from 1999 to 2003, earning three trips to the Pro Bowl during that period. After spending one forgettable season with the Cleveland Browns and another with the Detroit Lions, Garcia agreed to a one-year contract with the Eagles as a backup to Donovan McNabb.

When McNabb went down, Garcia assumed the reins of the offense with a no-nonsense, do-anything-to-get-the-job-done approach. The Eagles lost a lopsided game to the Indianapolis Colts the week after McNabb's injury, dropping the team's record to 5–6. But the season turned around the following week, in a Monday night game against the Carolina Panthers. With his team down by seven, Brian Westbrook put the Birds on the board with an eight-yard touchdown grab in the second quarter. The Panthers went back on top with a Keyshawn Johnson TD reception, but the Eagles answered with a 30-yard touchdown pass from Garcia to Donté Stallworth. A David Akers field goal put the Eagles up for good in the fourth quarter. Garcia finished with 312 passing yards and three touchdowns.

Garcia led the Eagles to another win the following week. Philadelphia eked out the 21–19 victory against the Washington Redskins. But a bigger test approached: the Eagles had lost a tough game to the New York Giants in week 2 of the season. Now, if the Birds wanted a chance at the playoffs, the road led through Giants Stadium in East Rutherford, New Jersey.

By this time, the team appeared happy with Garcia at quarter-back. But the second game against the Giants would prove whether Garcia could still lead a team to victory in a big game. He did his part, throwing TD passes to tight end L. J. Smith and wide receiver Reggie Brown. But Brian Westbrook was the big story on offense.

He carried the ball 19 times for 97 yards, including two touchdowns, and he pulled down five passes for 40 yards. During the game, which the Eagles won by a score of 36–22, Brian surpassed the 1,000-yard rushing milestone for the season.

The Eagles closed out the regular season with wins against the Dallas Cowboys and the Atlanta Falcons. The team's 10–6 record was good enough to win the NFC East division and earn a playoff berth. The first-round opponent would be the New York Giants.

Quick but Queasy

The Eagles-Giants **rivalry** is the oldest in the NFC East division. The first meeting was in 1933. Over the years there have been some unforgettable moments. In 1960, for instance, Eagles' linebacker Chuck Bednarik blindsided Frank Gifford on a pass play, knocking the Giants halfback out cold. Gifford suffered a severe concussion that almost forced him into retirement.

CROSS-CURRENTS

Before the founding of the Eagles in 1933, Philadelphia had another professional football team. Read about the Frankford Yellow Jackets on page 52. ▶▶

During the November 19, 1978, game between the teams, the Giants led 17–12 and had the ball with only half a minute remaining. But rather than run out the clock by having quarterback Joe Pisarcik "take a knee," the Giants called a running play. The handoff to halfback Larry Csonka was fumbled, and Eagles cornerback Herman Edwards scooped up the ball and ran 26 yards into the end zone for a game-winning touchdown. The play, dubbed the "Miracle in the Meadowlands," is perhaps the most famous incident in the history of the Eagles-Giants rivalry.

Twenty-eight years after the Miracle in the Meadowlands, the Eagles were intent on gaining another victory at the Giants' expense. But midway through the second quarter of the January 7, 2007, NFC **wild card** game, their explosive running back developed stomach cramps. Although he had been an asset to the Eagles since joining the team, some critics continued to doubt Brian Westbrook's toughness. Now, in the middle of the most important game of the season, he felt queasy, weak, and out of breath.

Brian took a swig or two of medicine to calm his stomach and returned to the field. On the second play of the second quarter, with the Eagles parked at the Giants' 49-yard line, he ran Garcia's handoff in for a jaw-dropping touchdown. By game's end, Brian had rushed for a career-high 141 yards, and the Eagles had prevailed, 23–20. Offensive coordinator Marty Mornhinweg said later of Brian:

"He was hurting big time. I was concerned that he wouldn't be with us down the stretch there in that particular game, and he gutted it out. We gave the ball to him quite a few times there late in that game and he got the job done, and he was hurting pretty good."

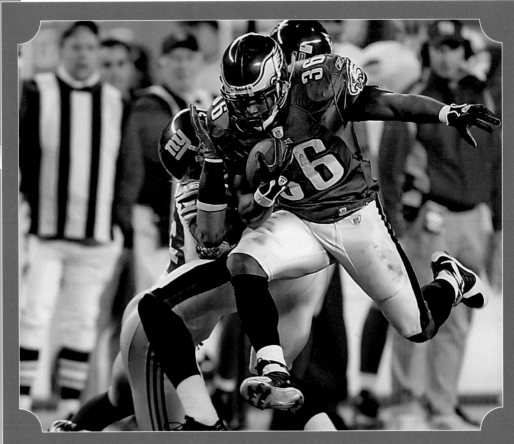

Despite suffering from flu-like symptoms during the game, Brian Westbrook powered the Eagles to victory in their NFC wild card matchup against the New York Giants on January 7, 2007. Brian carried the ball 20 times for a career-best 141 yards.

Hurting or not, Brian's gritty performance helped propel the Eagles deeper into the postseason. It also silenced those who doubted his toughness. When asked later about playing while sick, Brian simply said that he didn't want to disappoint his teammates.

Hold On

A week later, the Eagles played the New Orleans Saints in the divisional playoffs. As usual, Brian was in the middle of the offense. Near the end of the first half, with the Eagles trailing 13–7, Brian plunged into the end zone from one yard out, giving his team a one-point edge heading into the locker room at halftime. Then, at the beginning of the third quarter, Brian took a handoff from Garcia and raced 62 yards for another touchdown. The Eagles appeared on their way to winning the game. In the end, however, the Saints prevailed, 27–24. Brian finished the game with excellent stats: 116 rushing yards on 13 carries. But that wasn't what he focused on in the aftermath of the disappointing loss. Brian had dropped three passes, including one that would have led to a first down deep in Saints territory. Speaking to the media after the game, Brian readily owned up to his miscues:

> **"There are some plays that I definitely wish I could have back. There were some dropped balls, which were uncharacteristic of myself. And that's a thing when you're trying to win a football game, you can't have that. I wish I had those plays back."**

Still, the playoff defeat couldn't completely overshadow Brian's outstanding 2006 season. He had gained 1,217 yards on the ground—marking the first time in his career that Brian had rushed for over 1,000 yards—and his yards per carry average of 5.1 was outstanding. He had racked up an additional 699 yards on a team-high 77 receptions, and his 11 TDs also led the Eagles. There was little doubt the Eagles needed Brian Westbrook.

Quarterback Controversy

By season's end, the Eagles had a quarterback **controversy** on their hands. Coach Andy Reid remained publicly committed to Donovan

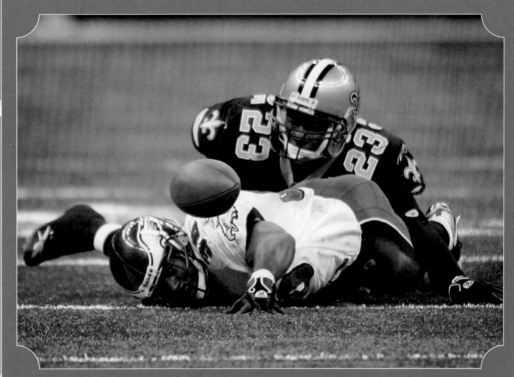

Although he scored two touchdowns—one on an electrifying 62-yard run—Brian Westbrook also dropped several passes in the Eagles' 27–24 divisional playoff loss to the New Orleans Saints. "There are some plays that I definitely wish I could have back," Brian told reporters afterward.

McNabb. But sports radio programs were abuzz with callers questioning McNabb's ability to lead. They saw a stark contrast between McNabb's easygoing, jovial demeanor and Garcia's hard-driving intensity. They also liked Garcia's attitude and his competitive spirit, two things some believed McNabb now lacked. While a few believed Garcia should replace the veteran quarterback, many others at least wanted Garcia signed for another season as McNabb's backup.

Going into the 2007 season, Donovan McNabb had played for eight years in an Eagles uniform. Over that period, he had racked up some impressive numbers, including 152 touchdown passes and an additional 24 rushing TDs. He was among the least-intercepted quarterbacks in NFL history, on average attempting more than 40 passes for each pick he threw. In addition, McNabb was only the second Eagles quarterback to lead his team to the Super Bowl. Nonetheless, his critics suggested that McNabb didn't play particularly well under pressure, and there was no denying that injuries had plagued him since 2005.

Few Eagles fans would have anticipated that Brian Westbrook might weigh in on the team's quarterback controversy. Unlike other

Donovan McNabb (left) and Jeff Garcia joke around during training camp in 2006. Before the season was over, McNabb had been injured and Garcia had stepped in to lead the Eagles to the playoffs. Yet the Eagles' front office declined to offer Garcia a contract for the 2007 season.

NFL stars, Brian has never been outspoken. Whatever opinions he has about the direction of his team, or the decisions of the Eagles' front office, he generally keeps to himself or expresses behind closed doors. But in February 2007, less than a month after the Eagles' playoff defeat in New Orleans, Brian talked publicly about Jeff Garcia's situation. During a radio interview in Miami, Brian complimented Garcia:

> **We've been saying it the whole time that Jeff has been playing that he's brought that fire back and he's brought that competitiveness back. He's a leader. He's a guy that guys follow, and everybody has played better since Jeff has gotten in there—and that's a real, true definition of a leader.**

Many fans wondered whether Brian's high praise of Garcia came at the expense of Donovan McNabb. Was Brian saying that Garcia was a leader while McNabb was not? Brian later denied that he had intended to slight McNabb. Instead, he voiced confidence in the Eagles' longtime quarterback. Brian also said he was hoping that the team would play more consistently in 2007.

In the end, neither Philly fans, nor radio hosts, nor even Brian Westbrook got to make the decision about who would play the quarterback position for the Eagles. Andy Reid and the Eagles' front office made that call. And their decision was not to offer Jeff Garcia another contract. Instead, A. J. Feeley was signed to a three-year deal as Donovan McNabb's backup.

As for Brian Westbrook, contract negotiations and a strong desire to get the Eagles back on track were foremost in his mind as the 2007 season approached.

STILL HUNGRY

After a frustrating 2006 season, the Philadelphia Eagles were looking ahead. With their quarterback controversy behind them, Donovan McNabb set to return to the lineup, and Brian Westbrook preparing for another thrilling year, the team was once again considered a Super Bowl contender.

CROSS-CURRENTS

In the NFL, reaching the top is hard. Staying there can be even harder. To read about some Super Bowl teams that have fallen fast, see page 52. ▶▶

Time of the Season

For week 1 of the 2007 season, the Eagles flew to Green Bay, Wisconsin, to meet the Packers at historic Lambeau Field. Things went wrong early on.

The Eagles and their star running back entered the 2007 season with great expectations. The team would falter, but Brian Westbrook's performance was nothing short of spectacular.

Taking the first punt of the game, Eagles receiver Greg Lewis fumbled the ball in his own end zone, resulting in a Packer touchdown. Still, the game remained close, and Brian Westbrook did his part by racking up 131 all-purpose yards. But mistakes, including a second fumbled punt and a Donovan McNabb interception, ended up costing Philadelphia the game, 16–13.

The next week, Philadelphia played its home opener in a *Monday Night Football* matchup against the division-rival Washington Redskins. The Eagles fans who packed Lincoln Financial Field had little to cheer about. Their team failed to get the ball into the end zone all night, and four David Akers field goals weren't enough to

The Eagles' offensive line opens up a big hole for Brian Westbrook in a game against the Washington Redskins. Once he gets past the line of scrimmage, Brian is one of the NFL's most dangerous runners.

win. Brian Westbrook rushed for 96 yards on 17 carries, and he pulled down 8 receptions for 66 yards, but the Redskins prevailed, 20–12.

On week 3 Philadelphia finally found its footing. Three minutes into the contest against the Detroit Lions, Brian Westbrook took a McNabb handoff and ran 25 yards into the end zone. As he had done so many times in the past, the back provided the Eagles' offense a spark. That spark quickly caught fire, as the Eagles scored touchdowns on their first five offensive possessions. On the second possession, Brian scored on a five-yard touchdown run. The next three drives were capped by Donovan McNabb TD passes to new Eagles receiver Kevin Curtis.

Late in the second quarter, Brian got his own TD reception, a 43-yarder. He finished the game, a 56–21 Eagles romp, with 110 rushing yards and 111 receiving yards.

Unfortunately, the Eagles couldn't sustain the offensive firepower they unleashed on Detroit. Against the New York Giants the following week, Philadelphia managed only a field goal in a 16–3 loss.

Brian Westbrook did his part to make sure the Eagles beat their next opponent, the New York Jets. Brian dashed for 120 yards on 20 carries, and Philadelphia won, 16–9.

But the team never managed to put together a winning streak. The week after their triumph against the Jets, the Eagles lost a 19–16 heartbreaker against the Chicago Bears, who scored the winning touchdown with just three seconds left on the clock. The Eagles bounced back from that defeat to down the Minnesota Vikings, 23–16. But then they fell to the hated Dallas Cowboys, 38–17, despite Brian Westbrook's first-quarter touchdown and 155 all-purpose yards in the game.

The seesaw season continued with a 33–25 win against the Washington Redskins in week 10. The following Sunday, against the Miami Dolphins, Donovan McNabb had to leave the game with a sprained ankle and an injured thumb on his throwing hand. His replacement, A. J. Feeley, kept the Eagles in the game, and Coach Reid relied on Brian Westbrook to pick up the offensive slack. Brian carried the ball a career-high 32 times for 148 yards. For the second week in a row, the Eagles came away with a victory, this one by the score of 17–7.

But three consecutive losses followed. In week 12 Philadelphia fell to New England, 31–28. Week 13 saw the Seattle Seahawks down the Eagles by a score of 28–24. The following week it was the New York Giants who handed Philadelphia a loss, 16–13.

The Eagles closed the season by winning three games in a row. But the team's 8–8 record wasn't good enough to earn a spot in the playoffs.

Seattle Seahawks safety C. J. Wallace goes airborne to stop Brian Westbrook from scoring, December 2, 2007. Seattle won the game, 28–24, dropping Philadelphia's record to 5–7. The Eagles would finish the year at 8–8.

Brian Westbrook had remained one of the few constants in the Birds' roller-coaster season. He finished the year with 1,333 rushing yards. He also caught 90 passes for 771 yards. His 2,104 total yards led the NFL. Ever dependable, Brian scored 12 touchdowns and fumbled only twice all season, despite handling the ball nearly 370 times. For his outstanding performance he was named to his second Pro Bowl and his first All-Pro Team.

All of Brian's hard work had added up to a season that at least one sportswriter referred to as one of the greatest ever for an Eagles running back. Yet for Brian, the individual glory was overshadowed by his team's dismal showing.

CROSS-CURRENTS

The Pro Bowl has special rules to minimize the risk that players will be injured. For details, see page 54.

Generous Spirit

Brian, like most of his teammates, keeps a strict workout regimen during the off-season. But the six months away from football also give him time to volunteer for a variety of charitable causes. Since his early days in the NFL, Brian has committed himself to doing good things for others. In 2003 he organized "The Westbrook Bowl," a celebrity bowling tournament that raises money for the Variety Club of Philadelphia, which provides services to children with disabilities throughout the Delaware Valley. Brian has also worked with the Police Athletic League (PAL) of Philadelphia by hosting street ball tournaments whose proceeds go to PAL.

But in May 2008, Brian tried something new by volunteering his time at the Bartrum and Brown Football Camp at Marshall University in West Virginia. He tossed passes, played quarterback, and even spoke to the campers about the hard work it takes to overcome adversity. According to campers and the other players in attendance, Brian's words struck a chord with the young people.

Weapons and Contracts

As a player who has proved his worth, and as a team leader who wants the Eagles to succeed, Brian has been a bit less shy to voice his opinions in recent years. In a recent interview, he spoke frankly about the strengths and weaknesses of the team. Like Donovan McNabb, Brian said that the Birds should acquire more big-time playmakers, especially on the offensive side of the ball. He cited the success of the Patriots as evidence that such an approach pays dividends:

> **"I think having more weapons on your team takes the pressure off of everybody. If you look at a team like the Patriots, they have so many weapons that if you shut down one guy, it just gives so many more opportunities to other guys to play well.**
>
> **If you have those guys who can make those plays, it makes it a lot easier on the entire team. That's something we could definitely use and hopefully we'll get that. "**

Despite their loss to the Giants in Super Bowl XLII, New England remains the gold standard for NFL teams looking to improve. But neither Brian Westbrook nor Donovan McNabb makes personnel decisions in the Eagles organization. That responsibility is left to Andy Reid and the team's front office. And while the club did sign a superstar free agent in the off-season, that player was a defensive specialist: cornerback Asante Samuel. Eagles decision makers declined to aggressively pursue a top-level receiver or another star running back. McNabb and Brian Westbrook, it seemed, would remain the club's only standout weapons on offense.

If his Eagles were apparently not going to have an additional offensive playmaker in the lineup, another concern of Brian's as he headed into the 2008 season was his own job. With three years left on his contract, Brian was apparently not satisfied with his pay. In 2008 Brian would earn $3 million. In 2009, if he remained with the Eagles, that number would rise to $3.5 million; the final year would bring him $4.5 million. While such numbers are staggering for the average person, they are not quite in alignment with the pay of elite running backs like LaDainian Tomlinson of the San Diego Chargers, who earns more than $5 million per season. Brian indicated that he would like the Eagles to renegotiate his contract:

CROSS-CURRENTS

NFL stars make a great deal of money. Information on contracts and salaries can be found on page 55. ▶▶

"I think if you play at a high level, you should be rewarded for that. You see guys that are the best players in the league, traditionally they're rewarded for their play. I feel . . . and I'm sure a lot of other players feel like they should be compensated for the things that they do.**"**

Asante Samuel (center) poses with head coach Andy Reid (left) and team owner Jeffrey Lurie at the press conference announcing the Eagles' signing of the free-agent cornerback, February 29, 2008. Samuel's six-year contract with the Eagles was reportedly worth $57 million.

Philadelphia Eagles players, team officials, and fans hope that the swift feet and sure hands of Brian Westbrook can help fulfill their dreams of a Super Bowl victory.

Looking Ahead

Recognizing Brian Westbrook's importance to the team, Eagles officials did indeed offer him a new contract. On August 8, 2008, he agreed to a three-year deal worth at least $21 million.

The Eagles will probably continue relying on their star running back to generate much of the team's offensive firepower—for as long as he remains on the team and as long as he stays healthy. Aside from Donovan McNabb, Brian is arguably the only Eagle who is a consistent threat to break a routine play for a huge gain. This is due to his explosive quickness and his extraordinary ability to elude tacklers. These attributes, in turn, are a large part of the reason Brian has proved so durable even though he is undersized by the standards of NFL running backs. Whereas larger backs often plow into defenders head-on, Brian tends to use his shiftiness to make tacklers miss. For this reason he doesn't absorb as many big hits.

Brian long ago proved his early doubters wrong: he is, in fact, big enough, strong enough, and healthy enough to have a long and successful career as an NFL running back. He has already broken many Eagles team records, and before his career is through, he may well be considered the best running back in franchise history.

Yet personal glory remains secondary to the Eagles' superstar. Foremost in his mind is getting another shot at playing in the Super Bowl—and this time, winning a coveted championship ring. Until then, Brian says, he simply wants the chance to take the ball and make some magic.

"I always want the opportunity to have the ball in my hands to do the things I know I can do. I can make people miss. I can make plays. I can run inside. I can run outside. I can catch the ball."

Such play and such passion have been hallmarks of Brian Westbrook's career. Whether he likes it or not, Brian Westbrook is an NFL secret no longer.

High Time in Honolulu: The Pro Bowl

At the end of each football season, the NFL says "Aloha!" as the AFC-NFC Pro Bowl, featuring the league's best players, takes place in Hawaii. The idea of a game to showcase each season's gridiron greats began before World War II. On January 15, 1939, the NFL champion New York Giants met all-stars from a host of other professional teams in Los Angeles. The Giants won the day, 13–10, and the game's popular success prompted the league to make the Pro All-Star Game an annual event.

After the December 1941 Japanese attack on Pearl Harbor in Hawaii drew the United States into World War II, the game was moved to New York City amid fears that the West Coast was vulnerable to another Japanese strike. By 1943 the war had caused the cancellation of the All-Star Game entirely.

In early 1951, the NFL brought back its all-star contest. The game was played between the American and National Conferences between 1951 and 1953; from 1954 to 1970 the Eastern and Western Conferences faced each other.

Aloha Stadium in Honolulu, Hawaii, hosts the NFL's annual Pro Bowl. The game—which is played on the Sunday after the Super Bowl—pits the American Football Conference's best players against their counterparts in the National Football Conference.

In 1959 a rival league to the NFL, the American Football League (AFL), was founded. From 1962 to 1970, the AFL held its own all-star game. After the AFL merged with the NFL in 1970, the AFC-NFC Pro Bowl was born.

The system of player and coach selection is well established: The coaches of teams that lost the AFC and NFC Championship games lead their respective squads. Unlike baseball all-stars, who are voted on solely by fans, players for the Pro Bowl are chosen by fans, coaches, and the players themselves. Each group has a one-third voting power. (Fans can votes at www.nfl.com.)

Each Pro Bowl player uses his own team helmet, but to avoid confusion on the field, home jerseys are red for the AFC team and blue for the NFC squad. The away team wears white with red or blue accents. Uniforms are redesigned every two years. At the end of the game, a Most Valuable Player is named.

Although the outcome of the Pro Bowl doesn't count for anything—and the game has special rules to minimize the chances of player injuries—being selected is an honor. And during the week before the actual game, Pro Bowl players get the chance to relax in Hawaii, soak up the sun, and socialize with colleagues. This football holiday is, for many, a perfect way to end a hard-fought season. (Go back to page 6.) ◀◀

Philly: A Football Kind of Town

Philadelphia sports fans are renowned—some would say notorious—for the intensity of their passion. Opposing teams playing in the City of Brotherly Love can expect to be serenaded by a chorus of boos, along with all manner of jeers and personal insults. Underperforming Philadelphia athletes aren't spared the wrath of their fans, either. Some of the raw emotion stems from repeated disappointment: going into 2008, none of Philadelphia's major pro teams—baseball's Phillies, basketball's 76ers, hockey's Flyers, or football's Eagles—had won a championship in 25 years.

For loyalty, enthusiasm, and occasional misbehavior, the Eagles' faithful take a backseat to none of their Philly-sports-fan peers, or to the fans of other NFL teams. Some of their antics have passed into legend. In December 1968, fans pelted a man dressed as Santa Claus with snowballs. In 1989 snowballs—along with batteries and beer—rained down on the hated Dallas Cowboys and their coach, Jimmy Johnson. During a Monday night game against the San Francisco 49ers in 1997, controversial calls by the officials and the poor play of the Eagles fueled a series of fights in the stands, and one fan even fired a flare gun over the field. That debacle prompted the team and the city of Philadelphia to establish a courtroom at Veterans' Stadium to deal immediately with out-of-control or drunken fans. While the reputation—good and bad—of the Eagles-obsessed is well deserved, few American sports teams can claim fans with as much passion.

(Go back to page 9.) ◀◀

The NFL Draft

Each year the NFL conducts what is officially termed a *player selection meeting*, commonly called the draft. This is the process by which the NFL brings new players from the ranks of college football into the league.

The draft is organized into a series of seven rounds. In each round, each of the 32 NFL teams gets to pick a player. The order in which teams pick is determined by their success the previous year. The team with the worst record gets the first choice. The team with the second-worst record gets the second choice, and so on. The Super Bowl winner gets the last pick of the round. The draft is organized this way to try to balance the talent levels among the teams. Teams can change the order of their pick, however, if they trade a player. The Super Bowl winner, for example, could trade a star player for a higher pick.

The draft takes place near the end of April, and it is a huge media event. The top players usually attend and dress well for the event. Fans often boo or cheer a particular pick.

For NFL coaches and team executives, however, the hype is beside the point. Their focus is on getting the players who will most be able to help their team win. A good draft can greatly improve a team's performance—and in some cases, the improvement is immediate. On the other hand, several bad picks can hamper a club's chances for years to come.

Diamonds in the Rough

In the early years of the NFL, teams often did not know much about the players they drafted. They depended on word of mouth or phone calls to sportswriters or college coaches.

That is no longer the case. Scouting has become a science. Enormous files are maintained on prospects. Would-be draftees are weighed, measured, timed, and even given intelligence and psychological tests.

Most of the time, this homework pays off. A recent study of All-Pro players over the last five years showed that half were drafted in the first round.

Sometimes, however, players have slipped through the cracks. In the 2002 draft, for example, 90 players were selected before the Eagles finally chose Brian Westbrook in the third round. And occasionally, a player is completely overlooked on draft day, only to go on to have a Hall of Fame NFL career. Undrafted Hall of Famers include quarterback Warren Moon, and defensive backs Willie Brown and Dick "Night Train" Lane. (Go back to page 15.) ◀◀

Donovan McNabb

Philadelphia Eagles quarterback Donovan McNabb was born in Chicago in 1976 and went to Syracuse University. The Eagles made him the second player chosen in the 1999 NFL draft. McNabb has played in Philadelphia ever since.

Fans, players, and coaches voted McNabb into the Pro Bowl every year from 2000 through 2004. During those years, the team went to four NFC Championship games. After finally winning the Championship after the 2004 season, the Eagles reached Super Bowl XXXIX.

McNabb's best season was 2004, the season the Eagles went to the Super Bowl. This was the first year that he had wide receiver Terrell Owens available to catch his passes. During the regular season, McNabb completed 64 percent of his passes, threw 31 touchdowns, and ran for three other scores. His 104.7 passer rating—a statistic designed to measure a quarterback's efficiency—ranked fourth among NFL QBs. McNabb set the NFL record for most consecutive completed passes, throwing 24 over the course of two games. He became the first quarterback in league history to throw more than 30 touchdown passes and fewer than 10 interceptions in a season. (He was picked just eight times during the regular season.)

(Go back to page 21.) ◀◀

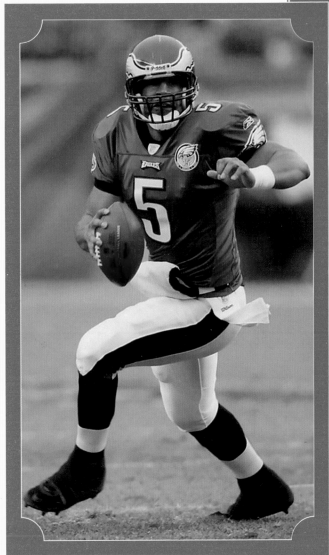

All-Pro quarterback Donovan McNabb has been guiding the Eagles' offense since 1999. McNabb was the first quarterback in NFL history to pass for more than 30 touchdowns while throwing fewer than 10 interceptions in a season. He accomplished the feat in 2004.

The Eagles' First Super Bowl

Twenty years is a long time if you are counting. And the Philadelphia Eagles and their fans had been counting since 1960, the last time the team had won a championship. But the 1980 Eagles and their intense head coach Dick Vermeil believed the long wait might finally be over. Led by quarterback Ron "Jaws" Jaworski and powerhouse halfback Wilbert Montgomery, the Eagles boasted a potent offense. But they were only half the story. The mean, green defensive machine led by nose tackle Charlie Johnson and linebackers Jerry Robinson and Bill Bergey typically crushed their opponents with a fierce pass rush and a wall of linemen. The Birds finished the regular season with a division-leading record of 12–4. They disposed of the Minnesota Vikings, 31–16, in the divisional playoffs, then thrashed the Dallas Cowboys, 20–7, to win the NFC Championship and earn a trip to the Super Bowl.

Their opponent in Super Bowl XV was the Oakland Raiders, whose main story during the 1980 season was quarterback Jim Plunkett. It

The Sporting News

SUPER BOWL
BOOK

1981

For Eagles fans, the Super Bowl XV story had a bad ending. Quarterback Jim Plunkett led his Oakland Raiders to a 27–10 victory over the Birds. It was the first time in NFL history that a wild card team had won the Super Bowl.

was widely believed that Plunkett, winner of the 1970 Heisman Trophy, was washed up. In fact, after five losing seasons with the New England Patriots and two more with the San Francisco 49ers, some said he had never lived up to his potential in the first place. By 1978 Plunkett had signed as a backup quarterback with the Raiders. He didn't see much playing time until starting quarterback Dan Pastorini broke his leg in the sixth game of the 1980 season. Plunkett eventually led the Raiders to victory in 9 of their last 11 games, earning them a wild card playoff berth. After beating the San Diego Chargers in the AFC Championship game, the Raiders became only the third wild card team to reach the Super Bowl.

Super Bowl XV was a lopsided affair. On the Eagles' first passing play, Raiders linebacker Rod Martin intercepted a Jaworski pass, running the ball 17 yards to the Eagles' 30-yard line. Jim Plunkett did the rest, throwing touchdown passes of 2 yards, 80 yards, and 29 yards—and earning Super Bowl MVP honors. Philadelphia's offense was smothered by the tough Raider defense, managing only one field goal and a late-game touchdown. The final score was Raiders 27, Eagles 10. For the Philadelphia Eagles and their long-suffering fans, the wait for another championship would continue. (Go back to page 22.) ◄◄

Wilbert Montgomery: Eagles Legend

The Philadelphia Eagles' first Super Bowl appearance, in January 1981, would not have happened without fleet-footed Wilbert Montgomery. On January 11, the running back had stuck it to the Dallas Cowboys in the NFC Championship game by rushing for 194 yards, including a 42-yard touchdown.

Born in Greenville, Mississippi, Montgomery played college ball at Abilene Christian University, where he started all four years and set a National Association of Intercollegiate Athletics record with 76 career touchdowns. He was picked by the Eagles in the sixth round of the 1977 NFL draft.

In all, number 31 played eight seasons for the Eagles, giving defenses nightmares along the way. In 1979 Montgomery led the NFL with 2,012 yards from scrimmage. He became the team's all-time leading rusher, with 6,538 yards on 1,465 carries, and he scored 58 touchdowns. Montgomery played his final season with the Detroit Lions in 1985.

In 1986, he was inducted into the College Football Hall of Fame. A year later, he became the first inductee of the Philadelphia Eagles Honor Roll. He is widely considered one of the greatest players in Eagles history. "He wasn't real big," says former teammate Mike Quick, "but he was as tough as anybody to play that position. He hit guys in the chest. Guys would smash him, and he'd get right up, straighten his helmet, and be ready to play."

(Go back to page 29.) ◄◄

Early Eagles: The Frankford Yellow Jackets

Philadelphia is a city of neighborhoods, from Chinatown to Kensington, from Port Richmond to Chestnut Hill. The city's first professional football team, the Frankford Yellow Jackets, was born in just such a community.

The Frankford Yellow Jackets joined the NFL in 1924, but the team's origins can be traced to the Frankford Athletic Association beginning in 1899. Located in the northeastern part of Philadelphia, Frankford was home to many working-class citizens and included many athletes. The athletic association the members created ultimately promoted a baseball team, which won a city championship in 1905; a soccer team; and a football team that would one day become professional. The early days of the Yellow Jackets included two games on weekends—a home game on Saturday and an away game on Sunday.

The Great Depression brought financial ruin to the team, which played its last game on October 25, 1931. Two years later, businessmen Bert Bell and Lud Wray bought the franchise and changed the team's name to the Philadelphia Eagles. In its first few years of existence, the Eagles wore the same light blue and yellow jerseys of the Frankford team. On September 23, 2007, the Philadelphia Eagles took the field in replicas of those same uniforms as a tribute to the Yellow Jackets of long ago. (Go back to page 30.) ◀◀

Staying on Top

In professional sports, reaching the top is difficult—but staying there can be even harder. There are a variety of reasons for this. First, opponents have no trouble getting pumped up to play a defending champion; everybody wants to beat the best. Second, winning a title requires intense dedication and focus. Many athletes find it harder to make the necessary sacrifices after they get a championship ring, and champions have to deal with more distractions, such as increased media attention. Success can also breed dissension, as players with big egos move to take credit for the team's triumph. And free-agent stars tend to go where the money is best, so owners typically must be willing to pay high salaries in order to keep their championship teams intact.

The NFL is no exception. Many teams have played in the Super Bowl only to have a dismal season the following year. In February 2007, for example, the Chicago Bears played in Super Bowl XLI, but next season they posted a losing record, finishing at 7–9. The same thing had happened to the Philadelphia Eagles after their appearance in Super Bowl XXXIX: the Birds managed to scratch out just six wins during the 2005 season.

Both teams that played in Super Bowl XXXVII posted losing records and failed to make the playoffs the following season, 2003. The defending champion Tampa Bay Buccaneers staggered to a 7–9 record. The Oakland Raiders fared even worse: the 2002 AFC champs got pushed around like chumps in 2003, managing to win only four games and tying several other teams for the worst record in the league.

The list goes on. The St. Louis Rams played in Super Bowl XXVI in 2002 but had a losing record the next season. The year before, the New York Giants suffered a 7–9 record after appearing in the Super Bowl.

But NFL free falls began long before the tribulations of these recent Super Bowl participants. In fact, the penthouse-to-doghouse storyline goes back almost to the beginning of the big game itself. The Green Bay Packers won Super Bowls I and II but then saw their dynasty abruptly end. Green Bay went 6–7–1 and failed to make the playoffs in 1968.

Another team that made NFL history suffered a similar fate. The Oakland Raiders became the first wild card team to win an NFL championship when they defeated the Eagles in Super Bowl XV. But that triumph was followed up with a disappointing 7–9 regular-season record in 1981, and the defending champs failed to make the playoffs.

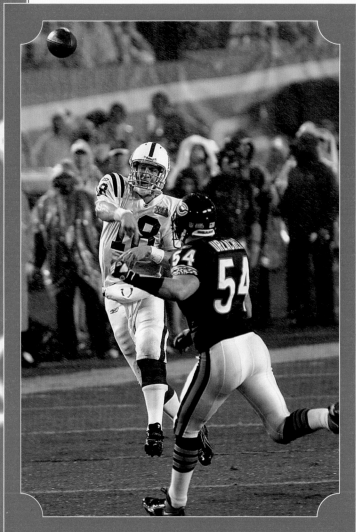

Chicago Bears linebacker Brian Urlacher chases Indianapolis Colts quarterback Peyton Manning during Super Bowl XLI, February 4, 2007. The season after appearing in the NFL's title game, Chicago failed to post a winning record.

(Go back to page 36.) ◀◀

Pro Bowl Rules

The Pro Bowl has been called the least intense game on the NFL schedule. Still, there is always the chance that a player might get seriously injured during the game, so the Pro Bowl is played under a special set of rules.

Under Pro Bowl rules, the offense isn't allowed to shift before the ball is snapped. The offense also is not allowed to send a receiver in motion, and it has to have a tight end on every play. The offense can't line up more than three receivers on one side.

To protect the quarterback, the defense isn't allowed to blitz. The defense is also required to line up in a 4-3 formation on every play, and it can't use more than four defensive backs to cover receivers. Unlike in regular-season games, the quarterback is free to throw the ball away, without penalty, if all of his receivers are covered.

Place kickers and punters are also protected under Pro Bowl rules. The special teams can't rush a kicker during a field goal attempt, on a punt, or during a point-after-touchdown (PAT) kick. A fan watching the Pro Bowl won't see any blocked kicks.

While you're not likely to see any bone-jarring hits during the Pro Bowl, you will see the best players in the NFL play an entertaining, wide-open, high-scoring, end-of-the-season exhibition game. (Go back to page 41.) ◀◀

Running back Adrian Peterson of the Minnesota Vikings, playing for the NFC, puts a move on AFC defenders during the 2008 Pro Bowl. The Pro Bowl game has special rules to minimize the risk of injury to players.

Money and the NFL

In the early days of professional football, players took the field for little more than a "sawbuck"—$10—and a pat on the back. But over the last 30 years, with the arrival of players unions and televised games, salaries have skyrocketed.

In 1994, in an effort to slow the rise in player salaries and to help owners control costs, the NFL put in place a salary cap for its players. This means that no team can spend more than a specified amount of money to pay the salaries of all the players on its roster. At the outset, the cap was set at $34.6 million annually. The cap is adjusted each year based on the amount of money the NFL earns. As of 2008 it stood at $116 million.

To afford their high-performing playmakers, team presidents craft complex contracts, which typically include bonuses, options, and deferred payments that spread costs out over a number of years in order to allow the team to meet a given year's salary cap. According to *Sports Illustrated*, four of the five highest-paid players for 2008 were quarterbacks. At the top of this list was Peyton Manning of the Indianapolis Colts, who received $18.7 million in compensation that would count toward the salary cap. New England Patriots QB Tom Brady was next, at $14.6 million. The two next highest paid quarterbacks were Carson Palmer of the Cincinnati Bengals (nearly $14 million) and Eli Manning of the New York Giants ($12.9 million). Defensive end Julius Peppers of the Carolina Panthers, the only non-QB in the top five, was the third highest paid player in the NFL, according to *Sports Illustrated*. Peppers received $14.1 million in compensation for 2008.

In all, a dozen players collected more than $10 million each toward their team's salary cap in 2008. Of course, they were some of the league's top stars, and the average NFL salary is considerably lower. The minimum salary for an NFL rookie in 2008 was $295,000. Each year of experience in the league guarantees a larger minimum salary.

Still, payroll costs for NFL teams are enormous. About two-thirds of all revenue generated by NFL teams each year goes to the players. In May 2008, NFL commissioner Roger Goodell announced that the league might extend the 16-game season by one game to increase team owners' profits.

(Go back to page 42.) ◀◀

1979 Brian Westbrook is born on September 2 in Washington, D.C.

1997 Graduates from DeMatha Catholic High School in Washington, D.C. In his senior year, is selected as first-team All-League and first-team All–Prince George County in football.

Enters Villanova University in Pennsylvania in the fall and plays on football team.

1999 Misses the entire football season because of injury.

2001 Finishes college football career with 9,512 all-purpose yards, an NCAA record.

2002 Drafted by Philadelphia Eagles in third round.

2003 Finishes the season with 11 touchdowns in backup role, but misses the playoffs because of injury.

2004 In first season as an Eagles starter, rushes for 812 yards and catches 73 passes for 703 yards.

Eagles reach the Super Bowl but lose to the Patriots.

Brian is named to his first Pro Bowl.

2005 In November Brian signs a five-year contract extension.

Has his best season yet, but misses the last four games of the season with a foot injury.

2006 Becomes the first Eagles running back to rush for 100 yards in three straight games since Wilbert Montgomery in 1981.

Finishes the season with 1,217 rushing yards, a career best.

2007 Finishes the season with 1,333 rushing yards; his 2,104 total yards leads the NFL.

Is named to his second Pro Bowl and first All-Pro team.

2008 In August, agrees to a new three-year contract with the Eagles worth at least $21 million.

Career Statistics

				Rushing					Receiving					Fumbles	
Season	Team	G	GS	Att	Yds	Avg	Lng	TD	Rec	Yds	Avg	Lng	TD	FUM	Lost
2007	Eagles*	15	15	278	1,333	4.8	36	7	90	771	8.6	57T	5	2	1
2006	Eagles	15	14	240	1,217	5.1	71T	7	77	699	9.1	52T	4	2	2
2005	Eagles	12	12	156	617	4.0	31	3	61	616	10.1	62	4	–	–
2004	Eagles	13	12	177	812	4.6	50	3	73	703	9.6	50	6	1	1
2003	Eagles	15	8	117	613	5.2	62T	7	37	332	9.0	38	4	3	2
2002	Eagles	15	3	46	193	4.2	18	0	9	86	9.6	20	0	2	2
	TOTAL	85	64	1,014	4,785	4.7	71	27	347	3,207	9.2	62	23	10	8

*Philadelphia Eagles

Accomplishments

2001   Walter Payton Award

2004   Pro Bowl

2007   First team All-Pro; Pro Bowl

Books

Didinger, Ray, and Robert Lyons. *The Eagles Encyclopedia*. Philadelphia: Temple University Press, 2005.

Gordon, Robert. *Game of My Life: Philadelphia Eagles—Memorable Stories of Eagles Football*. Champaign, IL: Sports Publishing, 2007.

Gordon, Robert. *The 1960 Philadelphia Eagles: The Team That They Said Had Nothing but a Championship*. Champaign, IL: Sports Publishing, 2001.

Silverman, Steve. *The Good, the Bad & the Ugly Philadelphia Eagles: Heart-pounding, Jaw-dropping, and Gut-Wrenching Moments from Philadelphia Eagles History*. Chicago: Triumph Books, 2008.

Web Sites

http://www.philadelphiaeagles.com

The official Internet home of the Philadelphia Eagles features a team history, the current roster, news stories, and more.

http://www.bwestbrook.com

The personal Web site of Brian Westbrook offers statistics, a photo gallery, a brief biography, and information on the running back's charity work and personal appearances.

http://www.nfl.com

The official Web site of the National Football League.

http://www.bleedinggreennation.com

Philly fans love their "Iggles," and this Web site is only further proof. Although the site contains team rosters, season schedules, and player statistics, its best feature is the running blog. On it crazed and half-crazed Eagles fans can discuss the team until they are blue—or green—in the face.

http://www.insidetheeagles.com

"Inside the Eagles" claims it is the top Eagles fan site on the Web. It includes game summaries, merchandise, and a weekly sports question for fans to vote on.

backfield—typically the halfback and fullback, who line up behind a quarterback before the beginning of a play.

controversy—a public dispute, debate, or quarrel.

franchise—the right or license granted by a company to an individual or group to market and sell its products.

gridiron—nickname for the field on which a football game is played.

interception—a pass that is caught by a member of the defensive team, thereby resulting in a change of possession of the football.

media—members of the press, including television, radio, newspaper, magazine, and Internet reporters.

NCAA—the National Collegiate Athletic Association, which governs college athletics in the United States.

rivalry—competition between people or teams.

suburb—a district outside of a city or town.

wild card—one of two teams in each of the NFL's conferences that makes the playoffs without winning its division.

Chapter 1: A Secret No Longer

page 6 "When you're getting voted . . ." Quoted in Bob Brookover, "Westbrook, Andrews Selected to Pro Bowl," *Philadelphia Inquirer*, December 19, 2007, E01.

page 8 "I think the more . . ." Quoted in Bob Brookover, "Westbrook Makes Rounds as Media Star," *Philadelphia Inquirer*, January 31, 2008, E07.

page 9 "When I see the two . . ." Ibid.

Chapter 2: DC to the Main Line

page 13 "Bill McGregor and his assistant . . ." Quoted in Coach McGregor's All Star Football Camp. http://www.coachmcgregor.com

page 15 "He's an every-down back . . ." Quoted in Jere Longman, "Who Knew Brian Westbrook Could Run, Receive and Return?" *New York Times*, February 1, 2005. http://www.nytimes.com/2005/02/01/sports/football/01eagles.html

page 15 "He's a heck . . ." Quoted in Steve Patton, "Will Westbrook Play?" *Reading Eagle*, September 25, 2007. http://andy-reid-news.newslib.com/story/3503-2835929/

Chapter 3: Small but Tough

page 19 "He respects his players . . ." Quoted in Mark Maske, "Eagles Follow Reid's Game Plan," *Washington Post*, January 26, 2005, D01.

page 22 "He creates so many . . ." Quoted in Longman, "Who Knew Brian Westbrook Could Run?"

page 22 "He's been doing a great job . . ." Quoted in Nunyo Demasio Tarik-El, "Foes in Md. High Schools, Teammates in Philadelphia," *Washington Post*, February 3, 2005, D01.

Chapter 4: We Can Rebuild Him

page 31 "He was hurting . . ." Quoted in Marc Narducci, "Fleet Westbrook Also Proves Tough . . ." *Philadelphia Inquirer*, January 11, 2007, D01.

page 32 "There are some plays . . ." Quoted in Bob Brookover, "Punting, 5 Critical Plays Did Birds In," *Philadelphia Inquirer*, January 16, 2007, D01.

page 35 "We've been saying it . . ." Quoted in Bob Brookover, "Westbrook Clarifies Remarks on Garcia," *Philadelphia Inquirer*, February 3, 2007, E06.

Chapter 5: Still Hungry

page 42 "I think having more . . ." Quoted in John Smallwood, "Eagles—Westbrook: Birds a Few Weapons Short," *Philadelphia Daily News*, January 31, 2008. http://www.philly.com/philly/sports/20080131_Eagles__Westbrook__Birds_a_few_weapons_short.html

page 43 "I think if you play . . ." Quoted in Bob Brookover, "High-Flying Westbrook Not Pushing for a Raise," *Philadelphia Inquirer*, June 10, 2008, D2.

page 45 "I always want . . ." Quoted in Ray Parrillo, "Westbrook's Numbers

Prove He Is a Workhorse," *Philadelphia Inquirer*, December 31, 2007, C07.

Cross-Currents

page 51   "He wasn't real big . . ." Quoted in Ashley Fox, "Wilbert Montgomery," *Philadelphia Inquirer*, August 12, 2007. http://www.philly.com/philly/sports/eagles/anniversary/20070812_inq_sports_ESIX.html

Numbers in **bold italics** refer to captions.

David Robson is an award-winning writer and English professor. He is the recipient of a National Endowment for the Arts grant and two playwriting fellowships from the Delaware Division of the Arts. An avid football fan since boyhood, he watched his beloved Philadelphia Eagles lose Super Bowls in 1981 and 2005. He dreams of the day when the Birds finally win the big game, but he won't hold his breath. David lives with his wife and daughter in Wilmington, Delaware.

PICTURE CREDITS

page

5: Barbara Johnston/Philadelphia Inquirer/MCT
7: Philadelphia Eagles/SPCS
8: Ron Cortes/Philadelphia Inquirer/MCT
11: Vicki Valerio/Philadelphia Inquirer/KRT
12: Fox Chase Cancer Center/PRMS
14: Villanova University Archives/AASI
17: Barbara Johnston/Philadelphia Inquirer/MCT
18: George Bridges/MCT
20: Eric Mencher/Philadelphia Inquirer/KRT
23: Bill Cummings/WireImage
24: Patrick Schneider/Charlotte Observer/KRT
27: Philadelphia Eagles/NMI
28: Ron Cortes/Philadelphia Inquirer/MCT
31: Ron Cortes/Philadelphia Inquirer/MCT
33: Jerry Lodriguss/Philadelphia Inquirer/MCT
34: Don Fisher/Allentown Morning Call/MCT
37: Philadelphia Eagles/SPCS
38: Rob Kandel/Allentown Morning Call/MCT
40: Ron Cortes/Philadelphia Inquirer/MCT
43: Philadelphia Inquirer/MCT
44: Ron Cortes/Philadelphia Inquirer/MCT
46: Zack Everson/SPCS
49: Kirby Lee/NFL/SPCS
50: The Sporting News/NMI
53: Terry Gilliam/MCT
54: James E. Foehl/U.S.DoD/NMI

Front cover: Ron Cortes/Philadelphia Inquirer/MCT
Front cover inset: Bill Cummings/WireImage